dingles&company

How to Make a Wormery

Leonie Bennett

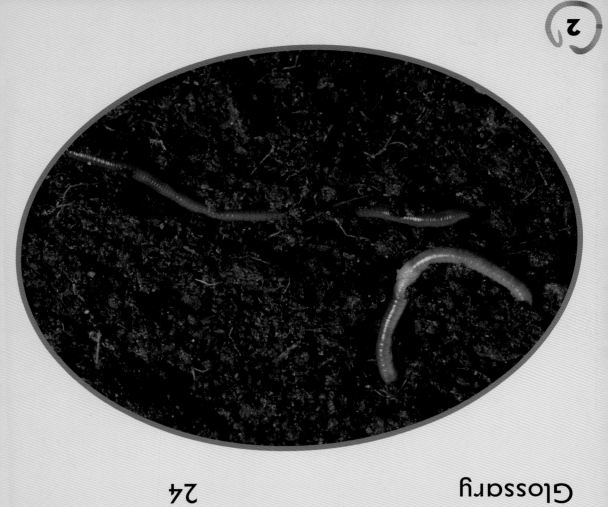

Contents

Introduction

Worms can make interesting pets.
It is easy to make a home for worms.
The home is called a **wormery**.

What you need

tank

black paper

sticky tape

soil

sand

- an old fish **tank** (or a big jar)
- some soil
- some **compost**
- some sand
- worm food, such as dead leaves or grass cuttings
- thick black paper
- sticky tape

grass cuttings

dead leaves

compost

What to do

tank

1. Put layers of soil, compost and sand into your tank.

soil

2. Put in some water if the soil is dry. The soil must be **damp**, but not too wet.

water

grass

leaves

compost

sand

3. Then put some leaves and grass on top.

4. Dig in the soil in the garden. Find some worms. You will need about ten for your wormery. Dig them up carefully.

Tip
Look for worms just after it has rained. Then the worms come to the top of the soil.

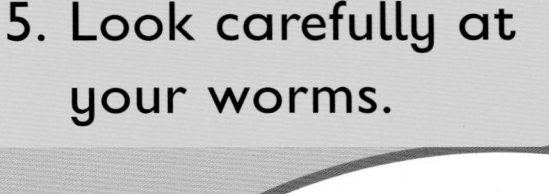

5. Look carefully at your worms.

- What color are they?
- Are some bigger than others?
- Do they look the same all the way along?
- What pattern can you see on them?

6. Then put the worms into your wormery.

7. Put some black paper on the sides of the wormery.
This will make it dark. The worms will think they are underground!

8. Then put your wormery in a **cool** place.

9. Leave the wormery for a few days.

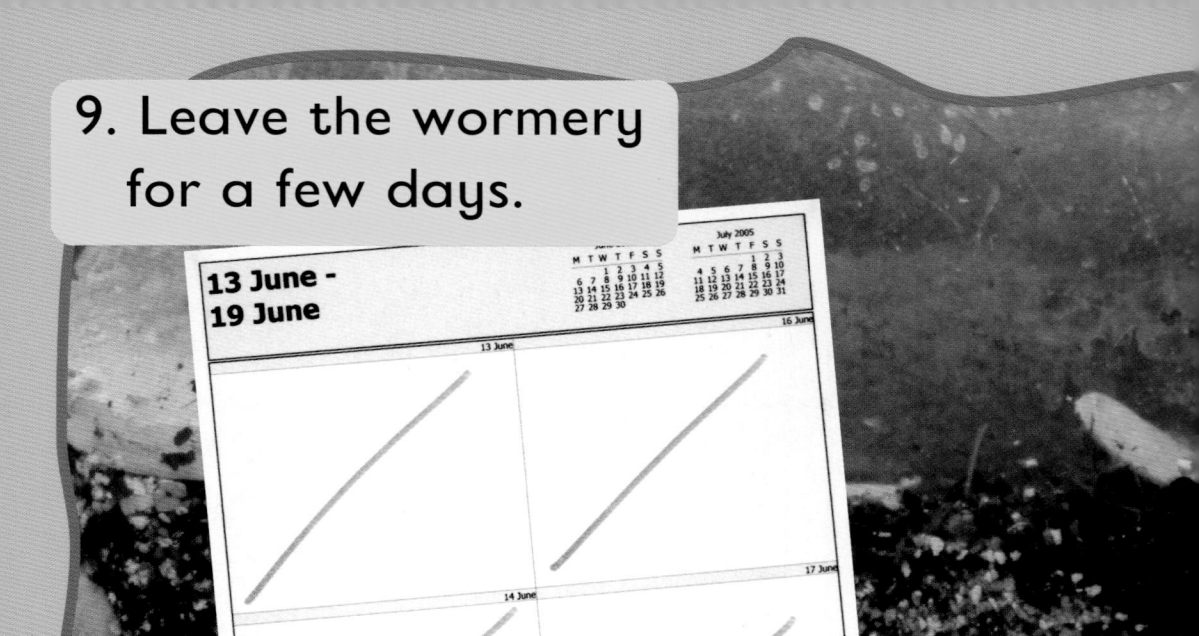

13 June – 19 June

July 2005

13 June
14 June
15 June
16 June
17 June
19 June

10. Then take a look.

1. What has happened to the layers of soil and sand?
2. What has happened to the leaves?
3. What else can you see?
4. What do you think the worms have been doing?

soil and sand

tunnel

mixed layers

buried leaves

12. Take a look every few days.
You will learn a lot about
how worms live and eat.

11. Add water to keep the
soil damp, but do not
make it too wet.

The worms have been eating the soil.

They have made **tunnels** in the soil.

They have pulled down the leaves and grass.

The worms have mixed up the layers of soil and sand.

Some things to try

1. Put potato peelings, tea leaves or orange peel on the top of the soil.
What happens to them?
What do the worms like best?

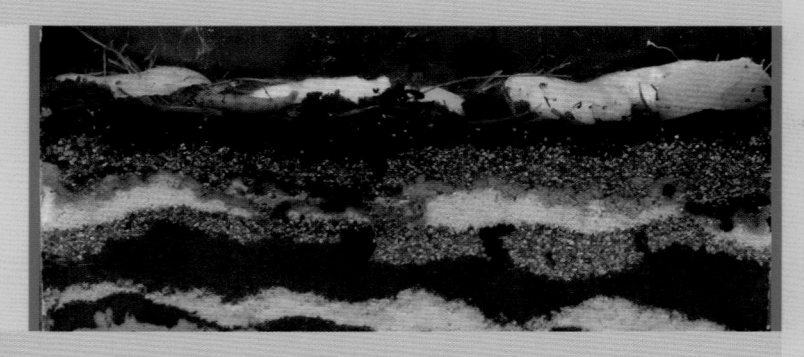

2. Look for **worm casts** on the top of the soil.
What do you think they are?

3. Put water on the soil.
What do the worms do?

4. Make a loud noise.
What do the worms do now?

13. After about two weeks, put the worms back in the garden.

The worms will mix up the soil and pull down dead leaves. They will help to put air and water into the soil. All this will help the plants to grow.

21

spade

Facts about worms

- Worms breathe through their skin.

- If a worm's tail is cut off, it can grow a new one.
It cannot grow a new head.

- Worms don't have eyes, but they move away from light.

- If a worm's skin dries out, it will die.

Glossary

Cool not warm

Compost a crumbly mixture of old leaves and plants

Damp slightly wet

Tank a large container

Tunnel an underground passage

Underground under the surface of the earth

Worm cast a small pile of soil that has passed through the worm (worm "poo")

Wormery a special place for keeping worms